A CATHOLIC PR[A] COLORING BOOK

FOR CHILDREN UNDER THE AGE OF 8

WITH EXTRA BLANK PAGES

ANDREA MARIE

This Coloring Book belong to

_____

Sign of the Cross

In the name of the Father, and of the Son, and of the Holy Spirit. Amen.

Our Father

Our Father, who art in heaven, hallowed be thy name. Thy kingdom come. Thy will be done, on earth as it is in heaven. Give us this day our daily bread; and forgive us our trespasses, as we forgive those who trespass against us; and lead us not into temptation, but deliver us from evil. Amen.

Hail Mary

Hail Mary, full of grace, the Lord is with thee. Blessed art thou among women, and blessed is the fruit of thy womb, Jesus. Holy Mary, Mother of God, pray for us sinners, now and at the hour of our death. Amen.

GLORY BE

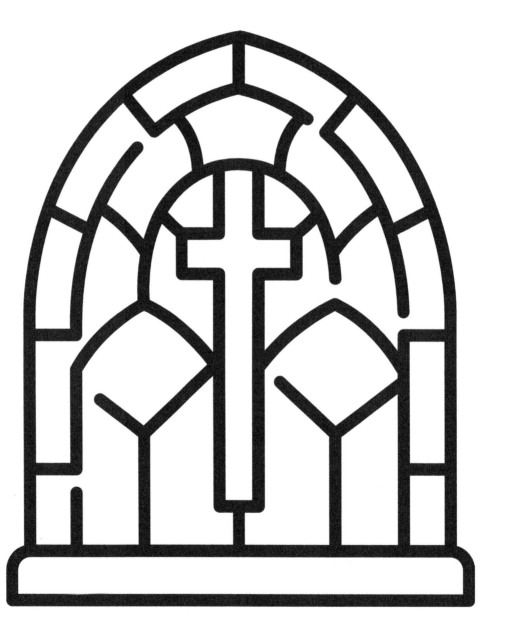

GLORY BE TO THE FATHER, AND TO THE SON, AND TO THE HOLY SPIRIT. AS IT WAS IN THE BEGINNING, IS NOW, AND EVER SHALL BE, WORLD WITHOUT END. AMEN.

ST. MICHAEL PRAYER

ST. MICHAEL THE ARCHANGEL,
DEFEND US IN BATTLE.
BE OUR DEFENSE AGAINST THE
WICKEDNESS AND SNARES OF
THE DEVIL.
MAY GOD REBUKE HIM, WE
HUMBLY PRAY,
AND DO THOU,
O PRINCE OF THE HEAVENLY
HOSTS,
BY THE POWER OF GOD,
CAST INTO HELL SATAN,
AND ALL THE EVIL SPIRITS,
WHO PROWL ABOUT THE
WORLD
SEEKING THE RUIN OF SOULS.
AMEN.

Guardian Angel Prayer

Angel of God,
my guardian dear,
To whom God's love
commits me here,
Ever this day,
be at my side,
To light and guard,
Rule and guide.
Amen.

TABLE BLESSING

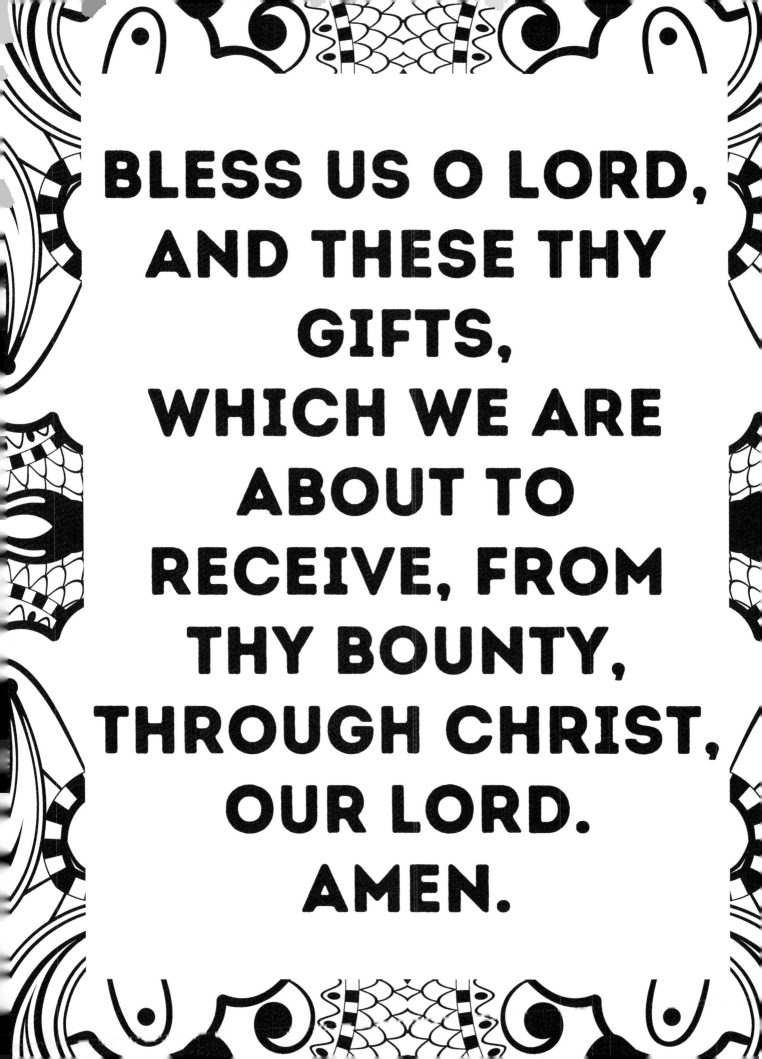

BLESS US O LORD, AND THESE THY GIFTS, WHICH WE ARE ABOUT TO RECEIVE, FROM THY BOUNTY, THROUGH CHRIST, OUR LORD. AMEN.

THE APOSTLES CREED

I believe in God the Father Almighty, Creator of Heaven and earth, and in Jesus Christ, His only Son, our Lord, Who was conceived by the Holy Spirit, born of the Virgin Mary, suffered under Pontius Pilate, was crucified, died, and was buried.

He descended into Hell; the third day He arose again from the dead; He ascended into Heaven and is seated at the right hand of God the Father Almighty, from thence He shall come to judge the living and the dead.

I believe in the Holy Spirit, the Holy Catholic Church, the Communion of Saints, the forgiveness of sins, the resurrection of the body, and life everlasting. Amen.

ACT OF CONTRITION

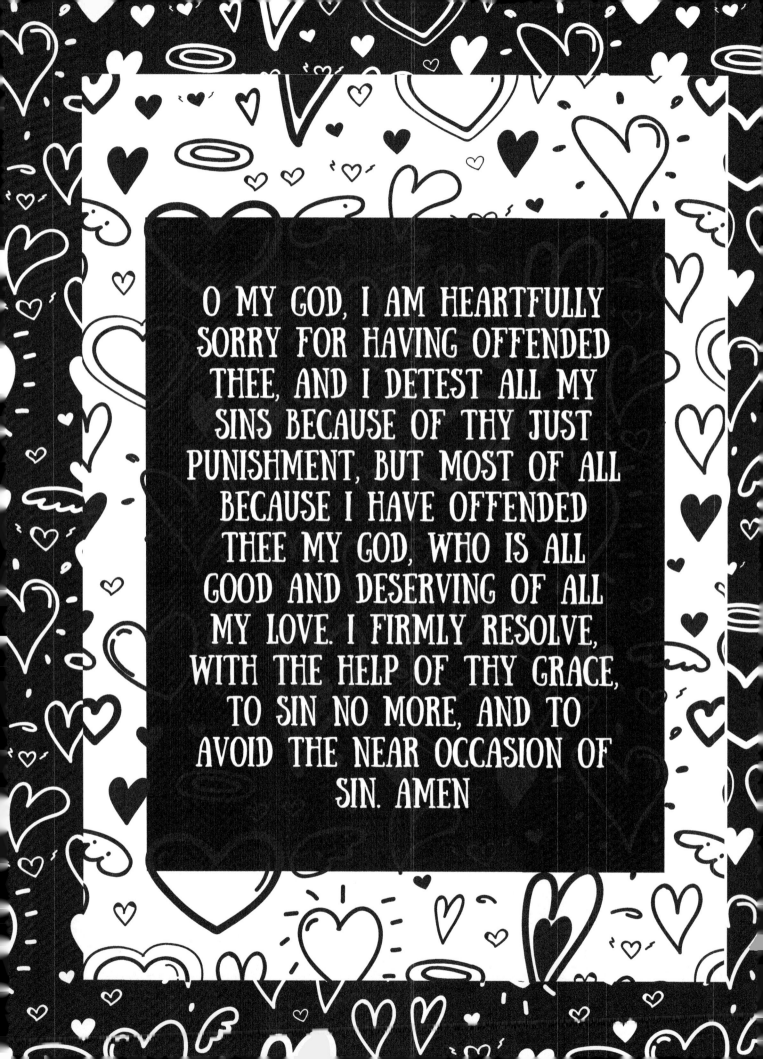

O MY GOD, I AM HEARTFULLY SORRY FOR HAVING OFFENDED THEE, AND I DETEST ALL MY SINS BECAUSE OF THY JUST PUNISHMENT, BUT MOST OF ALL BECAUSE I HAVE OFFENDED THEE MY GOD, WHO IS ALL GOOD AND DESERVING OF ALL MY LOVE. I FIRMLY RESOLVE, WITH THE HELP OF THY GRACE, TO SIN NO MORE, AND TO AVOID THE NEAR OCCASION OF SIN. AMEN

THE JESUS PRAYER

O LORD JESUS CHRIST, SON OF GOD, HAVE MERCY ON ME, A SINNER, AMEN.

Printed in Great Britain
by Amazon

40677605R00031